Transcendental Meditation: A Personal Journey

By Donald Emerson Crim PhD

ISBN: 978-0-615-27920-6

Printed in the United States of America

First Printing

<u>Table of Contents</u>

INTRODUCTION
(By Curtis Crim)

This text was written by Dr. Donald Emerson Crim PhD prior to his death on August 18th, 2007. It is about the experiences of him and his wife in the Transcendental Meditation movement and their year at Maharishi International University in 1983 and 1984. Many things have changed since this text was written, so I am writing this introduction to clarify references to some of these.

Maharishi International University has since changed its name to the Maharishi University of Management. The university has been working very hard to bring the architecture of the campus up to the standards of Stahpatya Veda. The pods have all been demolished, as has the Annapurna dining hall.

The people who run MUM are creative and motivated, so life and customs on campus change quickly. Keep this in mind when reading this text; you would do well to put differences between MIU of the past and the current state of MUM and the Transcendental Meditation movement into the context of the quickly-evolving TM movement.

SIXTEEN YEARS IN THE TM MOVEMENT

There is a tradition in anthropology of semi-disengagement from fieldwork experiences, a setting of limits of personal involvement, both temporal and geographical, which allows the anthropologist to keep the field and the home base fairly neatly compartmentalized. My involvement with the Transcendental Meditation movement does not allow for this sort of neat distancing, the separation of professional and personal roles. My family and I did not get into TM in order to study it ethnographically; rather, the impulse to do an anthropological study came more than seven years after we had become involved personally. Therefore, in this essay, you will find the personal and the professional closely intertwined. This procedure is not without its risks, in that when I recount the various stupidities that I committed while engaged in the doing of TM, you may wonder whether these were the result of personal lapses in judgment, or professional incompetence.

HOW WE GOT INTO THE TM
MOVEMENT

Back in the late 1960s, when I was a much
more recent member of the Colorado State
University anthropology department, I was
teaching AP 100, just as I am today. My
wife Pat and I were much involved with the
students who attended my classes and her
voice lessons (she taught in the Music
Department). In those days, we brewed our
own beer, mainly because we liked
entertaining lots of people for a small cost (1
1\2 cents a bottle!) And so, once or twice a
week, we would have humongous
home-brew parties at our house. In the
course of these, we got acquainted with many
of our students. Two of these were a couple
of guys who did Transcendental Meditation,
and who were really enthusiastic about it.
We were impressed with these guys, and
wanted to know more about this technique.
They encouraged us to attend introductory
lectures on TM, which were held frequently
on campus. I attended one of these, and
convinced Pat that she ought to attend one
too. She did, and then we talked about going
through the seven-step process of becoming
transcendental meditators. Finally, in view
of the cost ($75.00 for the entire family), we
decided that we just couldn't afford it.

And there the matter stood for another six
years. Then, after seeing more notices

appearing announcing introductory TM lectures, I went to another introductory lecture, then the preparatory lecture, and then, once again, dragged Pat reluctantly to a repeat of both lectures. This time, we decided to go ahead and get initiated (even though the price had risen to $200.00.)

And so the next Saturday morning, we turned up at the appointed place, a meeting room in the Student Union building at UNC in Greeley, each carrying a new white handkerchief, three flowers, and three pieces of fresh fruit. After a brief interview with the instructor, I was taken by him into another room, where there was a kind of altar-like arrangement, consisting of a small table draped with a white cloth, on which there were two candles, a picture of an Indian holy man (this turned out to be a likeness of Guru Dev, Maharishi's teacher), and several small brass containers. It was explained to me that I didn't have to do anything but stand and listen to the ceremony, and that at one point in the proceedings, I would hear a short phrase which would be my personal mantra, to be learned and used in meditation. This, indeed, is exactly what happened; the instructor began chanting in Sanskrit, while manipulating the various objects on the table (which included the handkerchief, fruit, and flowers that I had brought.) Finally, I heard the instructor repeating a short two-syllable phrase, which I recognized as the promised mantra.

As soon as the short ceremony (called the Puja Ceremony) was over, I was taken into another room and told to meditate, using my new mantra, for about twenty minutes. It was emphasized that this form of meditation was a simple, natural process, easy enough for anyone to do, and without any strain or effort on the part of the meditator. One simply sat comfortably, closed one's eyes, and silently repeated the mantra. If and when one's attention drifted away from the mantra, one simply and gently came back to it. After the twenty minutes were up, one sat quietly without repeating the mantra for a few minutes, in order to "come out of it" a sort of bringing the metabolism up to normal functioning after meditation, and a return to normal awareness.

Now why, you ask, would anyone want to engage in this practice (aside from the obvious fact that it is a restful process)? As was explained in the introductory lecture, the process of meditation is indeed restful; in fact, the rest gained is claimed to be much deeper that ordinary resting, or even sleeping. In addition, during meditation, stresses are released from the nervous system (harmlessly fizzing off like bubbles in a glass of Coors Light), stresses which are seen as a major source of unhappiness and confusion in one's daily life. Not only are recent stresses released (the rude driver encountered on campus, the fight with your companion the night before) but even ancient stresses (the time you were punished unjustly at age three for something you big brother did.) It was claimed that the regular twice-daily practice of TM would result in a whole series of improvements in your life, from better grades in school and better relations with those around you to greater success in any endeavor you might undertake, as well as the clearing up of minor problems such as insomnia, an over-fondness for home-brew, or a regrettable tendency to become enraged at inanimate objects, for example.

At the same time, our two children (Dorothy, age 16 and Curtis, age 14) agreed to be initiated. After a few weeks, they both lost interest in meditating, and stopped doing it for several years.

And so, we began to be regular meditators, with our twice-daily periods of meditation. Some results were immediate in coming; I began to sleep better almost immediately. Pat and I soon noticed that we were drinking less and less, partly because the evening meditation had taken over the time slot for Happy Hour, but more basically, because beer and wine stopped tasting very good.

We also gave up cigarettes, without any struggle. Other events followed our new practice as meditators; that summer was loaded with medical emergencies. I went to the hospital with severe abdominal pains, and was diagnosed as diabetic. While I was at PVH, Dorothy fell out of a tree and broke her ankle. It was explained to us by friends who had been in the Movement for longer than we that this was not unusual for new meditators; what we were experiencing was simply a release of accumulated stresses, a release which manifested itself in these various bodily symptoms and conditions.

Having enjoyed our meditations, and having experienced at least some of the promised results, we found that we wanted to know more about TM, the technique, and the movement (since it was obvious that there were many other meditators around in Fort Collins, and well as elsewhere in the country. There was a local TM center just north of the CSU campus, where regular "advanced lectures" were held, free to the TM public. We attended a series of these programs which consisted primarily of group meditations, followed by listening to and watching taped lectures by Maharishi.

The local center was directed by a young couple who were certified TM instructors. In addition, they held regular quarterly celebrations (at the equinoxes and solstices), which were covered-dish suppers followed by candle-lighting ceremonies celebrating the continual successes of the Movement, and the corresponding growth of enlightenment of society at large. We found that there was a lively "esprit de corps" among the local meditators, an enthusiasm for doing TM, an enjoyment of each other's company, and a sense of being involved in what was, for many meditators, a kind of holy crusade to improve the quality of life on the planet.

As time passed, we became more involved in TM activities. We were encouraged to attend a residence course, a three-day program for meditators at which we would do group and individual meditation, hear lectures on various aspects of the teachings, and learn some new techniques which, it was claimed, would increase the effectiveness of our meditations. These techniques consisted of some specialized breathing practices (Pranayama) and a series of postures (Asanas) derived from the Indian practice of Yoga (Asian Indian, not American Indian).

About two years later, Maharishi announced that a new program of advanced meditation would be made available to the TM faithful, a program called the TM Sidhis Program. Unlike many of the other programs offered, this one would take weeks of special training (with the final two weeks in residence at Maharishi International University at Fairfield, Iowa), and cost a cool $3000 per person (no family discounts here). It was claimed that not only would this practice speed up the evolution of the individual toward personal enlightenment, but also, the individual would actually learn to levitate!

Truth to tell, I had serious doubts about such claims; I may be old and fat, but not actually stupid. Nevertheless, based on glowing accounts of wonderful experiences enjoyed by those who had taken this training, and thus become sidhas, we decided to take the course of training. Needless to say, we did not, in fact, experience levitation, although we did find that some of the other problem areas of our lives began to smooth out after we became sidhas, including our children gradually pulling out of their Teenage Crazies and returning to their meditation practice. Both of them went on to become more involved with the Movement than Pat and I did; Dorothy subsequently spent ten years on Capital Staff at MIU, earning tuition for her Sidhis course, and for her Teacher Training. After becoming a TM teacher, she met and married a man who is also a TM teacher; they are now the directors of the TM Center in Kansas City. Curtis, after a few years of fooling around at CSU, went to MIU and took his degree in computer science last June. He is now employed as an engineer by a software firm in Fairfield.

A YEAR IN THE LIFE

In 1983, becoming eligible for a sabbatical leave, I decided that it might be interesting to spend the year at Maharishi International University, in Fairfield, Iowa. The idea was to spend the year doing a study of the TM community there and possibly to work with MIU faculty, either in teaching or in research. After correspondence with the MIU Dean of Faculty, and getting my application for sabbatical leave approved by CSU, Pat and I set out to Fairfield, on a hot day in August. We had been at MIU previously, for the final two weeks of our Sidhis course, three years previously. We had been accepted to the Creating Coherence Program, and were to live on campus, in one of the old frat buildings. On this course, we were to spend about six hours a day on our TM-Sidhis programs (which were made longer and more complicated during our stay on the course). The most important part of our programs was the twice-daily visits to the Golden Domes of Pure Knowledge, where the sidhas gathered to their programs in groups. What time was left over from these activities were to be spent partly in doing volunteer work at the Capital (a minimum of four hours weekly was expected), and the remaining few hours in activities judged by the CCP Office to be sufficiently evolutionary. We were required to turn in a time sheet once a week,

13

accounting for all of our time when we were not actually engaged in doing our TM-Sidhis programs. I found that this requirement was a powerful stimulus to the writing of creative fiction, since apparently no one in the CCP office ever actually checked to see if one had been engaged in the activities reported on the weekly time sheet.

Our volunteer work assignments turned out to be some of the most enjoyable things we did that year; we were assigned to the Capital bakery, where under the direction of our daughter (who had become an expert baker while working in the bakery), we helped in turning out large quantities of fresh breads, rolls, muffins, pies cakes, and other such delectable comestibles daily. Pat and I had always loved baking, and here was the opportunity to do it on a grand scale. The bakery was a jolly place to work; the people who worked there (mostly volunteers) had a fun time sharing jests, jokes, and wisecracks collaborating on the day's baking tasks. Also, other people who worked in the building kept dropping by, drawn by the delicious smells, to see what was just coming out of the ovens, and to sample if possible. (It was always possible; we kept a pan of fresh baked goods on the counter beside a large dish of softened butter for these snackers.) Looked at objectively, the bakery was actually a rather dangerous place to work; one was always juggling large loads of pastry in hot pans while walking around on a floor which was frequently wet or greasy, while the constant presence of powerful machinery and sharp knives added other challenges. It is somewhat remarkable that no one sustained a serious injury (aside from occasional minor burns) during the months we worked there.

Pat and I had been assigned adjoining rooms in an old three-storey building that at one time had been the home of a fraternity, back in the Parsons College days. The rest of the rooms were assigned either to married couples, or to single mothers with no more than one child. We shared a common dining hall in the basement (for part of the year), and common bathroom facilities on each floor. Since these buildings had been designed for occupants of the same gender, there were no separate bathrooms. The possible awkwardness of chance encounters with opposite sex bathroomers was solved by the use of signs made from paper plates on the doors of the bathrooms; these had separate sectors labeled "men", "women", "couple", and "vacant". The idea was that before entering, you checked to see that the arrow pointed to "vacant", and then moved it to the appropriate sector. People remembered most of the time to manage the sign correctly, although an occasional slip might have quietly hilarious results.

Eating arrangements changed from time to

time; originally the single men and women on CCP ate in separate dining halls, while the couples ate with one group or the other. Later, the dining room in our building was opened, and the residents were allowed to dine there. During the 7000 course, most of the people in our building had to trudge to the other end of the campus to take their meals in one of the dormitories there, while we were allowed to continue to eat in the dining room of our frat, since we had volunteered to be the dining room managers. Probably the best dining times were those that took place while we and the others in the building had our own dining room; there grew up a real sense of family and enjoyment of each other's company. And yet, as is the case in most communal dining situations, there were stresses and hard feelings which arose in connection with sharing common dining facilities. Some people complained that others would deliberately leave evening program early in order to have first shot at the dessert table. One woman became enraged when another woman took large quantities of fresh fruit to her room for private consumption, despite the fact that the second woman was a fruitarian, and ate nothing else. The first woman became so upset that she actually wrote a letter to the Capital Governing Board complaining of this situation, thus compelling the Board to convene a hearing, calling the second woman in to account for her behavior. Another woman kept collecting desserts, and storing them in the large communal refrigerator in the kitchen area. She never ate these desserts, and so someone had to clean them out and throw them away from time to time, which she never seemed to notice. There was never, at any time, a shortage of food, nor did the diners have to pay by the meal. Somehow, it was always the dessert course that became the focus of people's weird food trips.

A TASTE OF UTOPIA

Clearly the most significant event of the year was the sudden organization of the 7000 Course. At Thanksgiving time in 1983, there was a big course somewhere in the Eastern U. S. which Maharishi actually attended. He was reported to have remarked casually during this course that it would be wonderful if the Movement could just get at least 7000 sidhas together in one place, in order to hasten the dawn of world peace. This was an extension of the Maharishi Effect, which asserted that meditators and sidhas, doing their programs together, would have a powerful effect on the surrounding environment, and causes such effects as lower accident rates, lower hospital admission rates, lower incidence of crimes, and a host of other such beneficial results. Among his close followers, there grew the idea that such a project would be possible, and could be carried out at MIU in Fairfield, over the Christmas holidays. A group telephone call announced this ambitious plan to the Faithful assembled in the Men's Dome on the MIU campus. There immediately arose an almost unbelievable ground-swell of enthusiasm among the MIU people, to bring this off in the four short weeks which lay between the phone call and the planned opening day of this gathering. Dubbed the

"Taste of Utopia" Course (also referred to as the "7000 Course", this would bring over 7000 people to the MIU campus, and to the town of Fairfield (population: about 11,000). Realizing that this influx would put a severe strain on the physical facilities, as well as requiring meeting and program spaces which were simply not present, the Fairfield TM community geared up for a massive effort to prepare for this huge event. (It should be noted that these preparations took place during a stretch of weather during which the daytime high temperatures rarely broke 0 degrees.)

For living accommodations, people who already occupied dormitory, frat, and pod space would be doubled up, and doubled up again. For example, a couple such as Pat and I, who had hitherto had one room apiece, would be separated into newly-created men's and women's floors and each of us would acquire from three to five same-sex roommates. A mobile-home court, holding about 50 units, was planned and built, even provided with underground plumbing. Town TM people were pleaded with to open their homes, and take in as many visiting Transcendental Meditators as they could stand. The two kitchens, one at MIU and the other at the Capital, made massive preparations to feed several thousand additional mouths. Food was ordered by the boxcar and semi-trailer load, menus were simplified, and additional dining halls were opened up in unlikely places. In order to provide more and larger meeting and program space, two buildings were quickly erected, barn-like structures of aluminum beams and corrugated aluminum siding, which could accommodate several thousand for programs or for meetings.

Maharishi had indicated that he would actually be in residence during most of the two-week course. This was seen as an unusual honor for MIU, since he had visited the campus only twice before, for brief periods. And, of course, very special preparations had to be made for his personal comfort. One of the frats, set aside for his personal use, was completely renovated, with repainting of all interior walls and ceilings, new carpets, and new furnishings. (In point of fact, the interior decor was redone three times in all; it seems that it took this many times to get it right.) Virtually everyone on campus (except the MIU students) was expected to take on additional duties during this period of frantic adumbrative activities.

I volunteered to work in an upholstery shop, located off campus, which had been entrusted with the awesome responsibility for providing the furniture for Maharishi's personal suite. This involved reupholstering existing furniture, and building other furniture from scratch. It seemed that

Maharishi has strong preferences for silk and satin upholstery, primarily in white, pink, and peach shades, and so fabrics satisfying these specifications were what we actually worked with. The hours were long, but the work was relatively easy. While I was driving staples through pink satin into hardwood (or into my thumb), Pat was part of a team that was preparing one of the frats for occupancy by Mother Divine, not a person, but a special, long-term group of female course participants, who live close to Maharishi, and frequently move to places within his immediate vicinity. This involved not only providing bedding and furnishings much more lavish than those provided to ordinary course participants, but also, refitting the kitchen so that the ladies of Mother Divine could do their own cooking, and stocking it with exotic foodstuffs (within the strictly vegetarian diet prescribed for those who stand high in the Movement hierarchy). The ladies of Mother Divine had a reputation for expecting maximum efforts to provide for their personal comfort, so that among the men who made daily deliveries to various parts of the campus, they were known as "Mother Demand". In all fairness, the Mother Divine ladies really had to depend on others to provide them with everything they might need or want, since they were not permitted to do any of their own shopping, or even have casual social contacts with other meditators on the MIU campus.

As preparations went frantically forward, there was very little evidence of shirking among the workers on or off the MIU campus; people worked long hours with reasonably good cheer. Some of the higher administrators even seemed to enter into unannounced but intense competitions to see who could work the longest in a continuous stretch; one high official was reputed to have worked for over 50 hours without sleep, meals, or even potty breaks, which I found hard to believe.

All of this required an additional ingredient, large sums of money. One of the wealthiest families in the TM community was said to have handed Bevin Morris (MIU president) a check for $6,000,000.00. Many other smaller contributors pitched in as well.

And before the last brush-load of paint had dried, or the last upholstery tack driven, the delegates began to arrive. People from all over the North American continent, and over fifty other countries, poured in. Particularly large delegations arrived from Germany, France, Japan, Israel, and Brazil. People were assigned accommodations without regard for their languages or national origins. Frat 114, where Pat and I had been living before the course had been planned, now became the temporary home for over 100 happy campers, from a wonderful variety of cultural backgrounds. She and I had volunteered to serve as frat managers, and well as dining room directors. What this meant is that we spent most of the time during the course arranging the dining halls and cleaning up after meals (and coping with a frequently-broken-down dish washer), as well as dealing with a large number of international guests who had pressing personal needs, but who for the most part did not speak English. We got to morning and evening programs usually, but rarely got to attend any of the other meetings.

Given the crowded accommodations, the bitterly cold weather, the less-than-inspiring menus (which leaned heavily on rice and dal, steamed broccoli, and cabbage casseroles), and the language barriers, it was remarkable that the delegates, for the most part, remained cheerful and agreeable, appearing to enjoy the huge group Sidhis programs (over 4000 men in the Grand Assembly Hall, on the average), and even larger communal meetings. Minor conflicts (over whether or not the windows should remain open at night in the bedrooms for example), were usually quickly and amicably resolved. Even obnoxious children were usually jollied out of their temper tantrums rather than threatened with severe bodily damage.

And did this huge convention bring world

peace? Not in any manner that was obvious to people outside the Movement, although the MIU press releases proclaimed a general easing of world tensions, and a variety of other indicators of reduced crime rates and rising prices of world stock exchanges. One entrepreneurial sidha in Fairfield, anticipating a steep rise in prices on the New York stock exchange during the course, encouraged several elderly sidhas to invest with him, with the promise of doubling their money in two weeks. In point of fact, the New York stock exchange, alone among the major stock markets in the world, failed to show the expected gains, and lost points instead. The elderly investors lost several thousands of dollars each, while the young entrepreneur simply shrugged it off. I suspect that the "bliss" which many of the participants claimed to experience throughout the course was more a function of almost everyone bearing the discomforts bravely, rather than mystical spin-offs from the huge group programs. It is interesting to note that on several occasions since 1984, the Movement has tried to get 7000 sidhas together for other huge courses, and has failed each time to attract anywhere near the magic number.

SUMMING UP

This essay had been a personal account of our family's involvement in the TM movement, and has avoided both the extravagant claims made by Movement functionaries, and the various occasions when the Movement has been "in the news". And yet, I would not want to leave you with the impression that the various members of our family are in complete agreement as to the claims made concerning the Movement's effectiveness. Clearly, Dorothy has made the greatest investment, both in time and labor, in the Movement, and is our only TM instructor. It is not surprising that she believes in the Movement most sincerely, having committed herself as a teacher and administrator, and having married a man who shares her views and commitment. Curtis, on the other hand, despite having spent over two years at MIU as a student, and having gotten heavily involved in the yearly Yogic Flying Olympics, found himself becoming more than a little disenchanted with life on the MIU campus. He found himself in occasional conflict with MIU administrators over what seemed to him to be ridiculous rules and regulations (such as the one that specified that a student could be denied graduation if he missed too many group programs in the Men's Dome). He also noticed that during these programs, there seem to have grown up a certain animosity between the non-hopping sidhas and the small group of Yogic Fliers, who quite naturally wanted to practice their Yogic Flying routines during the flying portion of the programs. Frequently, he would find upon entering the Dome that the specialized arrangements which he and the other Fliers had made for their practice had been taken apart by others. He even found occasional obscene messages attached to his backjack or blankets. It seemed strange to him that, while the top level of administrators (including Maharishi) made frequent public statements concerning the importance of doing the "flying" technique, the lower level administrators frequently appeared indifferent or hostile to the most active group of "fliers".

And what about the parents? Pat and I continue to do our TM programs on a daily basis (although occasionally taking liberties with cutting programs short in the press of other demands on our time). She is more strongly convinced than I that the sixteen years of our involvement has produced significant positive results in our lives, individually and as a family. And even I, the eternal skeptic, admit that our lives are much better than they were sixteen years ago, although it is hard to tell whether these improvements are the direct result of our TM activities. Maybe we continue to do TM as a matter of habit, as it is worked into our daily routines. Certainly I rarely if ever transcend during program. And even when I fall asleep during meditation instead of saying my mantra, those little naps can be mighty refreshing.

GLOSSARY

ASANAS: A series of postures and movements, derived from the Indian tradition of Yoga, said to increase the effectiveness of one's TM program.

CAPITAL OF THE AGE OF ENLIGHTENMENT (CAE). This is the administrative portion of the MIU (located on the northern half of the Campus) which sponsors and runs non-academics courses for TM people, ranging from weekend World Peace Assemblies to the Purusha and Mother Divine courses, which require a minimum of six years commitment.

CAPITAL STAFF. The group of administrators who run CAE, headed by the Capital Board, which consists of three married couples, who make all the policy decisions, and deal with all major interpersonal problems among the course participants.

CREATING COHERENCE COURSE (CCP). This is the course in which we participated during our year at MIU. It required a full twelve-month commitment on our parts in order that we would be eligible for the substantially reduced course rates

FRATS: One of the three principal types of residential architecture found on the MIU campus. The frats were oddly shaped buildings, each consisting of two two-storey octagonal units joined by a central two-storey unit consisting of a food-preparation and dining area on the lower floor, and a large meeting hall on the second.

MAHARISHI EFFECT, THE: In the middle 1970s, Movement publications began to proclaim the Maharishi Effect, based on a study carried out by Movement scientists. Using a matched set of cities in the US, one group of which had meditators making up 1% of each city's population, and the other group which did not, the study found that the 1% cities had a number of positive indicators of better quality of life, while the non-1% cities did not (Citation of materials from Vol. I of the Collected Papers). This provided the basis for the prediction that the 7000 course would have demonstrable effects on the entire population of the world.

MAHARISHI MAHESH YOGI: The founder of the TM Movement, and the original teacher of all certified TM teachers.

MANTRA: A short word or phrase in Sanskrit which is taught to the TM neophyte during the initiation ceremony. Non-Movement sanctioned publications carry what are claimed to be complete lists of Mantras. Such publications further claim that mantras are assigned purely on the basis of the age and sex of the neophyte.

MOTHER DIVINE: A course for female TM teachers, which requires a substantial commitment in time (six years minimum?), and a willingness to relocate frequently as the group moves around at Maharishi's behest.

During the year that we were a MIU, the Mother Divine ladies didn't appear to have much to do with the organization or work of the TM community; however, in more recent years, Mother Divine ladies have been assigned to important administrative positions.

PARSONS COLLEGE: When the Movement moved to Fairfield in 1974, they had purchased the old Parsons College Campus, which had stood vacant since Parsons College had gone bankrupt in 1972.

PODS: Another of the architectural styles in student housing on the MIU campus. The pods were small three-storey units, each storey containing six tiny one-person rooms and a common bathroom. During the 7000 Course, two people were assigned to each pod room.

PUJA: This ancient Hindu ceremony, which celebrates the glorious tradition of teachers who have passed on the Meditation technique, is performed each time a new person is initiated. It is also performed on numerous other occasions, especially when other techniques are being taught.

PRANAYAMA: A specialized breathing technique taught to new meditators on residence courses. It is supposed to increase the effectiveness of the meditation.

PURUSHA (THOUSAND-HEADED PURUSHA): The male equivalent of the Mother Divine Course. During the year we were at MIU, the Purushniks were widely considered to be the heroes of the Movement, since they had the reputation of being to cope with any emergency. The also had their own male chorus, quartet, and musical ensemble (which played a curious combination of Movement and Country music).

RICE AND DAL: Dal is a sort of thin vegetable curried mush, made from yellow mung beans, and served over rice. The degree of commitment of a TMer can be accurately measured by the degree of their enthusiasm for eating rice and dal over extended periods.

SANSKRIT: The ancient language in which the Vedas were written, the earliest language to be described in a linguistic text. It is claimed by TM linguists that Sanskrit is the original human language, and the only perfect language. Non-TM linguists have a hard time taking such claims seriously.

www.ingramcontent.com/pod-product-compliance
Lightning Source LLC
Chambersburg PA
CBHW060552030426
42337CB00019B/3525